M
GE

Travel Guide Book

A Comprehensive 5-Day Travel Guide to Munich,
Germany & Unforgettable German Travel

• *Travel Guides to Europe Series* •

Passport to European Travel Guides

Eye on Life Publications

Munich, Germany Travel Guide Book
Copyright © 2015 Passport to European Travel Guides

ISBN 10: 151860935X
ISBN 13: 978-1518609350

~

Other Travel Guide Books by
Passport to European Travel Guides

Berlin, Germany

Top 10 Travel Guide to Italy

Florence, Italy

Rome, Italy

Venice, Italy

Naples & the Amalfi Coast, Italy

Paris, France

Provence & the French Riviera, France

Top 10 Travel Guide to France

London, England

Amsterdam, Netherlands

Santorini, Greece

Barcelona, Spain

Istanbul, Turkey

Vienna, Austria

Budapest, Hungary

Prague, Czech Republic

Brussels, Belgium

"Germany often shines its very best in Munich."
—Dean Polk Shaw

Table of Contents

• Introduction •

Munich, Germany. A city steeped in rich, cultural history and recognized worldwide for its architectural gems. You may also be surprised to find a **bustling metropolis** here, full of some of Europe's most rousing and fascinating things to do and see. Visitors relish the beauty and simplicity of Munich.

From the annual Oktoberfest festivities, to the myriad of **elite museums** and **renowned theatres**, many consider the city of Munich to be one of the world's best places to call home!

In this 5-day guide to Munich, you'll find a variety of our top recommendations and helpful tips to prepare you for having the best travel experience in Munich! **Read over the insider tips** carefully and review the information on preparing for your trip. **Every traveler** has different tastes and budgets, so we've included a wide range of recommendations that include the best of everything.

You're welcome to follow our detailed **5-day itinerary** to the letter, or you can **mix and match** the activities and destinations at your own discretion.

Most importantly, we know you'll have a marvelous time in Germany!

Enjoy!

The Passport to European Travel Guides Team

• City Snapshot •

Language: German

Local Airports: Munich International Airport (MUC)

Currency: Euro | € | (EUR)

Country Code: 49

Emergencies: Dial 112 (all emergencies) 110 (police)

• Before You Go... •

✓ Have a Passport

If you don't already have one, you'll need to apply for a passport in your home country a good two months before you intend to travel, to avoid cutting it too close. You'll need to find a local passport agency, complete an application, take fresh photos of yourself, have at least one form of ID and pay an application fee. If you're in a hurry, you can usually expedite the application for a 2-3 week turnaround at an additional cost.

✓ Need a Visa?

The US State Department provides a wealth of country-specific information for American travelers, including **travel alerts and warnings**, the location of the **US embassy in each country**, and of course, **whether or not you need a visa** to travel there! http://travel.state.gov/content/passports/english/country.html

Additionally, you may also find **German visa information** for any nationality at: http://www.germany-visa.org

✓ Healthcare

The healthcare system in Germany is first-rate. **For visitors and non-residents**, neither emergency nor non-emergency treatment is free. Visitors from outside Europe will have to pay for any medical services and are advised to purchase a traveler's insurance *before* traveling to Germany and **be aware of what is and is not covered.**

Visitors from within Europe need to carry a valid **EHIC** (European Health Insurance Card) and present it at the time of treatment.

✓ Set the Date

We recommend traveling to Munich between **March and May.** Less crowds and better rates all around.

✓ Pack

• **We recommend packing only the essentials** needed for the season in which you'll be traveling. By far, the most important thing to pack is a good pair of **walking shoes** (water-resistant if you're traveling in colder months, and comfortable, light sandals or sneakers to walk good distances in warmer months).

• **Winter in Munich** can be well below freezing. So if you're budget traveling you may get the best deals on airfare, hotel rates, etc., but you'll need to pack thermal gear and heavy coats to survive the temperatures.

• If you're planning on visiting any **cathedrals or churches in Munich**, be sure to pack **clothes that appropriately cover** your shoulders and legs.

• We always recommend packing **hand sanitizer, sunscreen, sunglasses, a hat and umbrella or rain jacket.**

• **A backpack** can be handy during the day when you go out sightseeing and collecting souvenirs, particularly when getting on and off buses, boats, trains or trams.

• If you don't speak German, be sure to pack a good **conversational German phrase guide** to bring along with you. You'll find people a lot friendlier toward you if you don't go around assuming they speak your language.

• **Medication.** Don't forget to have enough for the duration of your trip. It's also helpful to have a **note from your physician** in case you're questioned for carrying a certain quantity.

• A simple **first aid kit** is always a good idea to have in your luggage, just in case.

• You can bring one or two **reusable shopping bags** for bringing souvenirs home.

• **Travelers from outside Europe** will need to bring along a **universal electrical plug converter** that can work for both lower and higher voltages. This way you'll be able to plug in your cell phones, tablets, curling irons, etc., during the trip.

• Be sure to **leave expensive jewels and high-priced electronics at home**. Like most major cities and tourist attractions, thieves and pickpockets abound. Avoid making yourself a target.

• **Take pictures of your travel documents and your passport** and email them to yourself before your trip. This can help in the unfortunate event they are lost or stolen.

• **Pack well,** but be sure to leave room for souvenirs!

✓ Phone Home

Before your trip, add a travel plan to your cell phone bill — they're pretty inexpensive these days and will give you peace of mind that you'll always be able to phone home if need be. You can also buy a cheap, **pre-paid local phone or phone chip** for your phone — which also gives you a local phone number. **Calling cards** are used less and less these days, but they're also an option.

Free is always the best option. Several online services and mobile applications offer free or very inexpensive ways to communicate with others from Munich. Such services include: *Skype, Facetime, WhatsApp, Viber.*

✓ Currency Exchange

It is important to note that most bars and restaurants in Munich do not accept credit cards — **cash only**. So it is important to have enough cash on hand.

Germany uses the **euro** (€) as its currency (same for most of Western and Central Europe). Check out the

currency exchange rates prior to your trip. You can do so using **the following** or many other online currency exchange calculators, or through your bank. For the best rates, we recommend **waiting until you arrive in Munich** to buy euros. The best way is to use your debit card to get cash at an ATM, but there are currency exchange desks in the airports.

For current exchange rates visit:
http://www.xe.com/currencyconverter

Also, make sure your bank knows you'll be traveling abroad. This way you avoid having foreign country transactions flagged and declined, which can be extremely inconvenient!

✓ Contact Your Embassy

In the unfortunate event that you should lose your passport or be victimized while away, **your country's embassy** will be able to help you. Be sure to give your itinerary and contact information to a close **friend or family member**, then also contact your embassy with your emergency contact information before you leave.

✓ Your Mail

Ask a neighbor to **check your mailbox** while you're away or visit your local post office and request a hold. **Overflowing mailboxes** are a dead giveaway that no one's home.

• Getting in the Mood •

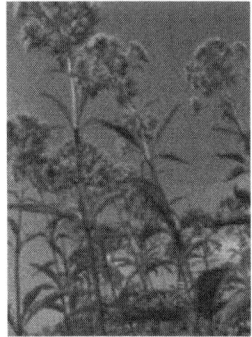

Here are a few great books and films set in or around **Munich** that we recommend you watch in preparation for your trip to this dreamy locale!

What to Read:

One awesome book we highly recommend before your trip to Munich is called, **The Book Thief** by Markus Zusak. It's the story of a 9-year old German girl, Lisa, just outside Munich. During WWII, Lisa was adopted. Her new parents were hiding a Jewish man named Max. When Max became very ill, Lisa would read a book to him every day and eventually began stealing books in order to continue reading to Max. A great read!

Another good book to read while traveling is **The White Rose** by Inge Scholl. In 1942, Hans Scholl and Sophie Scholl led an underground organization opposed to the heinous crimes committed by Hitler and his regime. The group called themselves *The White Rose*. They circulated information that clearly indicated they denounced Hitler's regime. Some of the group members were eventually caught and put to death.

What to Watch:

An important documentary that will have you on the edge of your seat is One Day In September, narrated by the legendary Michael Douglas. It's the true story of the Israeli athletes held hostage by a Palestinian group known as 'Black September' during the 1972 Olympics in Munich. It's definitely not one to miss!

A hilarious movie to get you prepared for your visit to Munich is **Beerfest,** starring Steve Lemme and Kevin Heffernan. **This is the story** of two brothers from the U.S. who find out about a century-old beer competition that happens during Oktoberfest in Germany. They lose so badly that they are determined to return in order to win the next time they compete. They organize a team of beer-lovers and return to Munich to join the competition again.

• Local Tourist Information •

The Munich Tourist Board is available to assist guests and provide helpful information related to local transportation, accommodations, healthcare, directions, banking and more. **The multi-lingual staff** is helpful and can share all about the most current events happening in the city at the time of your trip! Be sure to call ahead for current hours of operation.

http://www.bavaria.us/bavarian-cities-south-germany/a-munich-bavaria-germany

Munich Tourism Offices:

E-mail: Tourismus@muenchen.de
Phone Number: +49 (0) 89 233 96 500

Central Train Station
Location: Bahnhofsplatz 2, 80335, Munich

City Hall
Location: Marienplatz 2, 80331, Munich

• About the Airports •

The Munich International Airport is about 18 miles northeast of Munich and is the second busiest airport in the country. It features a visitor park with a play area and an 18-hole miniature golf course. **Terminal**

2 features a **Viewing Terrace** to watch planes arrive and take off. The S-Bahn railway will take you directly to the central station.

The airport is about 45 minutes drive from the city center.
http://www.munich-airport.de/en/consumer/index.jsp

• How Long is the Flight? •

The Flight to Munich:

- **From New York City:** approx. 8 hours

- **From Chicago:** approx. 9 hours

- **From Los Angeles:** approx. 11.5 hours

- **From Toronto:** approx. 7.5 hours

- **From Moscow:** approx. 11 hours

- **From London:** approx. 2 hours

- **From Paris:** approx. 1.5 hours

- **From Hong Kong:** approx. 12.5 hours

- **From Cape Town:** approx. 13.5 hours

- **From Sydney:** approx. 22 hours

• Overview of Munich •

Munich is a charming Bavarian city in Germany that rests along the **Isar River**. With a population of nearly 1.5 million residents, Munich is the capital and largest city of the German state of Bavaria, just north of the Bavarian Alps.

Well known for its captivating culture, stunning architecture, and yearly beer festival, **Oktoberfest**, most tourists are amazed to find a rather **cosmopolitan city** in Munich.

Although much of Munich was marred during World War II, many historic buildings still stand today, several having undergone **important restoration**, such as Munich's principal church, Frauenkirche.

Over the years, Germany's third largest city has not only become a **major metropolis** with lots of sophisticated dining and entertainment, but it's also **a dynamic city** that continues to forge ahead in the preservation of its distinctive culture.

A trip to Munich will open your eyes to a whole new fascinating world of discoveries we know you'll enjoy!

• Insider Tips For Tourists •

Etiquette

Overall, **German culture is rather formal** and exhibits a notably structured daily life. A quick, firm handshake is appropriate on greeting and departing, and it is best to use "Herr" and "Frau" (Mr. and Mrs.) with their last name until you are invited to use first names.

Germans also tend to be great planners, so if you make an appointment or reservation, you should **be on time**. Being a couple minutes late without notice can be considered very offensive. **When tardiness is unavoidable**, be sure to call and explain why you are going to be late.

Notes on dining out:

• **Most restaurants**, bars, pubs, etc., DO NOT accept credit cards.

• **When restaurants are busy**, it's common to share a table with people you don't know. A table labeled "Stammtisch" means the table is reserved so you should not sit there. **When seating yourself**, be sure to first ask whether or not the seat is taken ("Ist dieser Platz noch frei?" (Is this seat free?), and don't feel obligated to converse beyond a polite "Guten Appetit." **Always bid farewell** when leaving ("Auf Wiedersehen").

• **Water is usually not included** with the meal. You are always expected to pay for it.

• **In some establishments**, it's customary for the bread and butter to be added to the bill as a separate cover charge. Ditto for some familiar US fast food chains in Germany. Unlike the US, condiments like ketchup and mustard are usually not free.

Time Zone

Munich is in the UTC (universal time coordinated) + 1 hour time zone. There is a 6-hour time difference between New York City and Munich, Germany (Munich is ahead on the clock). When it is 8:00 am in New York City, it is 2:00 pm in Munich.

Saving Time & Money

Accommodations

• **We highly recommend** getting the **CityTourCard.** You can purchase it in advance on-line or at any tourist information desks, including those at the airport or central station when you arrive. **Admission to major attractions, discounts on tours and free access to public transit** are just some of the fantastic benefits:

http://www.mvv-muenchen.de/en/tickets-fares/tickets/day-tickets/citytourcard

• We also always recommend booking your **flight**, **hotel accommodations, show tickets,** transportation, etc. as far in advance as possible to avoid higher prices.

And if you can help it, **avoid traveling during the peak tourism season**, between June and August.

It is generally less expensive to stay at a hotel not located in or near the center of the city. Rates tend to be much lower when you stay at a hotel in a nearby suburb.

Dining

Many first-time tourists to Germany don't know that in many cases they can **bring their own food** to the beer gardens (biergartens), as long as you're buying drinks! And instead of eating in restaurants for every meal, why not check with the front desk of your hotel and ask for the nearest market and **spent less on food** options during your stay.

Sightseeing

If you are planning on visiting a few museums during your time in Munich, you can always do so on Sunday when admission is free!

Tipping

Wait staff in Germany are generally paid more than the US but are not reliant on tips for their salaries.

Service charges are typically included in restaurant bills, bar tabs, spa treatments, etc.

While a tip is not obligatory, it is the general practice to tip 5-10% for service and rounding up to the nearest whole number.

When You Have to Go

In Munich, public toilets are marked WC (water closet). In some cases the toilets may be unisex. If the toilet is gender specific, the door will have a symbol on it or read "Herrn" for men and "Frauen" for women.

When you need to go to the restroom you can ask: "**Wo ist die toilette?**"

Be sure to tip a few coins or euro to any **restroom attendants**, as they rely heavily on tips for keeping the restroom clean.

Taxes

Value Added Tax (VAT) a consumption sales tax throughout Europe. As of this writing, the standard rate in Germany is 19%. Reduced VAT rates apply for pharmaceuticals, passenger transport, admission to cultural and entertainment events, hotels, restaurants and on foodstuffs, medical and books.

Visitors from outside Germany may be eligible for a **VAT refund** if certain criteria are met:

1) you do not live in Germany

2) you must inform the retailer you are taking the goods out of the country. You will then receive "Ausfuhrbescheinigung" (export papers) or a **Tax Free Shopping Check** with your receipt

3) As you are leaving Germany you will need to **show the unopened, unused goods** at customs and have them **in your carry-on** since your bags will already have been checked. You will receive an export certificate.

4) If you have a Tax Free Shopping Check you may be able to **get your refund at the airport** if an office is available, otherwise the export certificate must be **sent back to the vendor** for the refund.

Phone Calls

The **country code** for Germany is 49.

When calling home from Munich, first dial 00. You will then hear a tone. Then dial the country code (1 for the U.S. and Canada, 44 for the UK, 61 for Australia, 7 for Russia, 81 for Japan, and 86 for China), then the area code without the initial 0, then the actual phone number.

To dial another local number in Munich, simply dial the number. The area codes are 2 digits but when you are dialing another district, let's say Berlin for example, you would dial 0 + the 30 area code. So from Munich to Berlin you dial: 030-234-4567.

Electricity

Electricity in Munich, as in the rest of Europe, is at an average of **220-230 volts,** alternating at about 50 cycles per second (to compare, the U.S. averages 110 volts, alternating at about 60 cycles per second.) As discussed before, when traveling from outside Europe you will need to **bring an adapter and converter** that enable you to plug your electronics and appliances into **the sockets** they use.

Cell phone, tablet and laptop chargers are typical]]ly dual voltage, so you won't need a converter, just an adapter to be able to plug them in. Most small appliances are likely to be dual voltage, but **always double check** when possible, especially to avoid frying hair dryers and travel irons.

In Emergencies

Emergency services are very efficient and prompt in Germany. **112 is the main emergency number** used throughout the European Union for all emergencies. Calls are answered in English, Italian, French, and German and routed to the appropriate unit.

In Munich specifically, you may dial 110 for the police.

German Phrases For Emergencies:

Help! = Hilfe!	
It's an emergency! = Es ist ein Notfall!	
Help me! = Hilf mir!	
Accident = der Unfall	
Fire! = Feuer!	
Where is a telephone? = Wo ist ein Telefon?	
Quick! = Schnell!	
I need a hospital. = Ich brauche ein Krankenhaus	
Where is the hospital? = Wo ist das Krankenhaus?	
I have diabetes. = Ich habe Diabetes.	
I am allergic to... = Ich bin alergisch gegen...	
There is an accident = Ein Unfall ist passiert.	
Call an ambulance = Rufen Sie einen Krankenwagen (Ambulanz)	

Holidays

Jan 1 — New Year's Day - National Holiday
Jan 6 — Epiphany - Common Local Holiday in some states
Feb 14 — Valentine's Day - Observance
Feb 16 — Shrove Monday - Observance
Feb 17 — Carnival/Shrove Tuesday - Observance
Feb 18 — Carnival/Ash Wednesday - Silent Day
Mar 20 — March equinox - Season
Mar 29 — Daylight Saving Time starts - Clock Change/Daylight Saving Time
Mar 29 — Palm Sunday - Observances
Apr 2 — Maundy Thursday - Silent Day
April — Good Friday – date changes from year to year - Silent Day
April — Easter Sunday - date changes from year to year - Silent Day
Apr 6 — Easter Monday - National Holiday
May 1 — May Day - National Holiday
May 10 — Mother's Day - Observances

May 14 — Ascension Day - National Holiday
May — Whit Sunday - date changes from year to year -- Silent Day
May — Whit Monday - date changes from year to year - National holiday
Jun 21 — Sunday- June Solstice - Season
Sep 23 — September equinox - Season
Oct 3 — Day of German Unity -National Holiday
Oct 25 — Daylight Saving Time ends - Clock Change/Daylight Saving Time
Oct 31 — Halloween - Observance
Nov 11 — St. Martin's Day - Observance
Nov 15 — National Day of Mourning - Silent Day
Dec 6 — Saint Nicholas Day - Observance
Dec 22 — December Solstice - Season
Dec 24 — Christmas Eve - Silent Day
Dec 25 — Christmas Day - National Holiday
Dec 26 — Boxing Day - National Holiday
Dec 31 — New Year's Eve - Observance

Hours of Operation

It's always important to plan ahead and make sure the places you want to go will be open on any given day. **On public holidays and Sundays** in Germany, most stores and shops are closed, with the exception of some in or near train stations. Most of the museums may open, but with limited hours, and likewise for public transportation.

Supermarkets in Munich are usually open: Mon.-Sat. 8:00 am - 8:00 pm

Department stores are typically open: Mon-Sat. 10:00 am - 8 or 9:00 pm

Banks are generally open: Mon.-Fri. 8:30 am - 4:00 pm, closed Sat. & Sun.

Money

As we mentioned, Germany's currency is the **euro** (€/ EUR) and, unlike many other countries, **credit cards are not widely accepted** in German restaurants, shops, bars and cafés. Some may accept them, but this is generally the exception.

It's best not to carry enough euros **in cash** to cover expenses, but try not to overdo it and carry too much money at any given time. In the event of loss or theft, this will minimize your damages.

It's best to utilize **ATMs** and tellers in the **non-tourist areas** of the city and be sure to use common sense and not make yourself a target for pickpockets. If an-

yone approaches you unexpectedly, it's best to polite-
ly keep walking.

Also, **beware the unnecessary fees.** If you're given
the option to pay in dollars vs. euros when using
your credit card, simply say no. Paying in dollars
will cost you more in fees and you may or may not
be informed of the additional charges at the time of
the transaction.

Climate and Best Times to Travel

Munich has an Oceanic Climate. If you want to avoid
the crowds and enjoy mild temperatures, **March,
April and May** are the ideal times for you to plan
your trip. Spring is in full bloom, the days are longer
and the temperature is milder.

May and June are particularly nice and **July** is usually Munich's warmest month. Summertime generally
isn't too hot, but it can be quite rainy, so don't forget
the rain jacket and umbrella.

If you are planning to visit Munich during Oktoberfest, keep in mind that you'll need to pack for temperatures between 40-50°F. While it is certainly a fun
and festive time to visit Munich, it can get a bit chilly.

Winter months can be below freezing.

Transportation

There are several ways to travel in Munich: *S-Bahn, U-Bahn, city bus, regional bus* and *tram.*

Public transportation is outstanding in Munich. With the **CityTourCard** you can ride free on most forms of public transit. A good place to start before you arrive is the **city's online planning tool**: http://www.muenchen.de/int/en/traffic.html

Driving

Although Munich is a very walkable city, there are times when you may prefer to drive.

Foreigners must be at least 18 to drive, and 21 to rent a car in Germany. Your US driver's license is valid in Germany for up to 6 months so no International Driving Permit (IDP) is needed unless you plan to stay in the country longer. If that's the case, **in the US**, AAA will provide you with one for about $10. You must also provide AAA with two passport photos.

Insurance is required and is available when you rent a car. Most driving rules are similar to the United States, however some notable differences are that officers can collect misdemeanor traffic fines at the time of writing a ticket. Also Germany has a Good Samaritan law that requires you to stop at an accident scene even if you're not directly involved.

If you are planning to drive in Germany you should do a bit more research to familiarize yourself with the traffic signs and other rules that may be different than those where you live.

• Tours •

Munich By Bike

Mikes Bike Tours are fun and lively. There are several packages to choose from, each one as exciting as the next. With small and more **intimate groups**, tourists get to experience the best of Munich without the distraction of a crowd. Tours usually last up to 4-hours and include at least one stop at one of the popular beer gardens.

Mikes Bike Tours
Address: Bräuhausstraße 10, 80331, Munich
Phone Number: +49 89 25 543 987
http://www.mikesbiketours.com/munich

Bike Munich is another great bike tour offered by Viator. This 3-hour tour takes you for a ride along the riverside to see the **medieval cultural center** and the city's most **picturesque gardens**. The tour eventually

stops at the popular Chinese beer garden where rid-
ers can socialize while drinking some of the city's
most impressive beers.

Bike Munich (Viator)
Phone Number: +888 651 9785
http://www.viator.com/tours/Munich/Munich-
Bike-Tour/d487-2666BIKE

Munich By Boat

Radius Tours offers our favorite and top recommen-
dation for a great way to see the splendor and charm
of this region of the world. Take a train just 30-minutes
outside of Munich to the beautiful **Chiemsee Lake** where
you'll board a boat to cruise to two lovely lakeside is-
lands. The tour also includes a stop at the **Herrenchiemsee Castle**.

Herrenchiemsee Palace and Boat Tour
Address: Arnulfstraße 3, 80335, Munich
Phone Number: +49 89 55 029 374
http://www.radiustours.com/en/english-
tours/herrenchiemsee-castle.html

Munich By Bus

Hop-On, Hop-Off Tours are the absolute best way to
see Munich by bus! Take in the sights that are of interest to you while allowing other tourists to go on to
points of interest to them. The Hop-On Hop-Off bus
tour in Munich offers two routes: the **Express route**

offers 6 points of interest and the **Grand Circle** tour offers 11 stops. These tours provide you all the flexibility you could ever want while touring, just hop on and hop off at your leisure!

Munich Hop-On, Hop-Off Bus Tours
Phone Number: +866 663 7017
http://www.hop-on-hop-off-bus.com/munich-bus-tours

Munich By Minibus or Car

Private Munich Sightseeing Tour offered by Viator takes you on a half-day tour of the city and a trip to the incredible Andechs Monastery. Your trip wouldn't be complete without a trip to a brewery along the way. Learn all you've ever wanted to know about Munich on this wonderful and private, 5-hour city tour.

Viator Private Munich Sightseeing Tour
Phone Number: +888 651 9785
http://www.viator.com/tours/Munich/Private-Tour-Munich-Sightseeing-Including-Andechs-Monastery/d487-2160ANDECHS

Try Special Interest or Walking Tours

SANDEMANs NEW Europe offers an awesome **3-hour walking tour** of Munich—for free! They cover all the top attractions and give a fabulous education about the city's traditions and history. Don't miss it!

SANDEMANs NEW Europe Munich | Free Walking Tour
Phone Number: +49 30 510 50030
http://www.newmunichtours.com/daily-tours/munich-free-tour.html

They also have a deliciously wonderful Bavarian Food Tour we highly recommend! Enjoy the great culinary culture with a taste of Munich. The tour lasts about 3 hours and you'll be whisked around to the best the city has to offer your tummy, from the farmer's market to the beer halls and upscale delis. Bon appetite!

SANDEMANs NEW Europe Munich | Bavarian Food Tour
Phone Number: +49 30 510 50030
http://www.newmunichtours.com/private-tours/bavarian-food-tour.html

Also, don't miss the wonderful Nuremburg Tour! Just a couple hours drive from Munich, it's an excellent day trip visiting the engaging city of Nuremburg. You'll spend about 4 hours experiencing the

city that was once center stage for the Third Reich—
and the Holy Roman Empire!

SANDEMANs NEW Europe Munich | Nuremburg Tour
Phone Number: +49 30 510 50030
http://www.newmunichtours.com/private-tours/nuremberg-tour.html

If you enjoy learning about the history of the destination you're visiting, you will definitely be interested in this historical walking tour. Although it takes tourists to a very unpleasant time in German history, **it's most enlightening** to see just how far Germany has come since those dark days.

Viator's Munich Third Reich Walking Tour offers two daily tours that educate tourists about the history of the dark days of Nazi Germany. The tour leads you to interesting historical sites that were of great significance during the reign of Adolf Hitler. You can take the 2.5-hour tour or the extended 4-hour tour, which includes an apartment of Hitler's. Just remember these are walking tours and they can be quite intense.

Third Reich Walking Tour
Phone Number: +888 651 9785
http://www.viator.com/tours/Munich/Private-Tour-Munich-Third-Reich-Walking-Tour/d487-2666REICH_P

• 5 Days In Munich! •

Enjoy this 5-day itinerary for a well-balanced and easy-going experience! Modify or adjust if you like! Also, be sure to **check websites or call ahead** for the most recent hours and pricing information. Enjoy!

• Day 1 •

We think the preferred way to experience Munich is most often on foot. So don't forget to pack your best walking shoes!

There's so much to see and do in Munich, and we want to make sure you get to as much as possible without tiring out too quickly. So we've created a **balanced suggested itinerary** that gives you **plenty of time to rest** in-between tours.

We suggest staying at a beautiful boutique hotel, **angelo Hotel Munich Leuchtenbergring**. Modern and upscale, it's the ideal place to stay since it offers quick access to the city center and major points of interest, like the **Bavarian Parliament** building and the **English Gardens**.

Upon arrival, if you've just had a long flight you may be inclined to simply settle in and do something a bit low-key on your first day in the city, which isn't a bad idea when you can have breakfast, lunch or dinner at the hotel's amazing **Restaurant Sunlight**.

Enjoy a meal at the hotel, then walk around the neighborhood a bit to get a feel for the area and to see where you can pick up public transportation.

Once you return from a nice, leisurely walk around the neighborhood, you can hit up the hotel lobby's bar, **Jazz**, while relaxing fireside with a cocktail.

Finally, it's off to bed for a restful night's sleep — tomorrow awaits!

Location Information:

angelo Hotel Munich Leuchtenbergring
Address: Leuchtenbergring 20, 81677, Munich
Phone Number: +49 89 189 086 0
http://www.vi-hotels.com/de/angelo-leuchtenbergring

Restaurant Sunlight
http://www.vi-hotels.com/en/angelo-leuchtenbergring/the-hotel/restaurant-sunlight

Jazz Bar

http://www.vi-hotels.com/en/angelo-leuchtenbergring/the-hotel/lobby-bar-jazz

• Day 2 •

After a nice breakfast at the hotel, begin your exploration of Munich at **Marienplatz**, the city's main square. A visit to the **Old Town Hall** is a must. It's gothic architectual design is world-famous to tourists interested in nice Kodak moments. You can easily spend a couple of hours here, making your way around to some of the interesting speciality shops, restaurants and attractions of Marienplatz.

Afterward, you can head over to the next city square, **Karlsplatz**. This square is known for its huge gothic gate and large fountain in the center. It is a great spot to people watch and grab a cup of coffee while taking in the sights and sounds of Munich. And by now, you may be hungry...

Stop into Conti Bistro, a trendy restaurant with a lovely atmosphere and surprisingly reasonable prices. However, if this setting is too formal for you for lunch, go there for dinner this evening and do **Mama Pizza** a fast, casual lunch.

At this point you've seen the attractions in two of the city's main squares and dined in a couple of its best eateries. Your exploration of Munich continues tomorrow!

Location Information:

Marienplatz
Address: 80331, Munich
Phone Number: +49 89 222 3324
http://www.muenchen.de/int/en.html

Old Town Hall
Address: Marienplatz 15, 80331, Munich
Phone Number: +49 89 233 9650
http://www.muenchen.de/sehenswuerdigkeiten/orte/120398.html

Karlsplatz
Address: Karlsplatz 80335, Munich
Phone Number: +49 89 515 5570

Conti Bistro
Address: Max-Joseph-Straße 5, 80333, Munich
Phone Number: +49 89 55 178 546
http://www.conti-bistro.de/de/home.html

Mama Pizza
Address: Augustenstr 16, 80333, Munich
http://www.mama-pizza.de

• Day 3 •

Today is sure to be an exciting day full of interesting things to see! After breakfast, let's start with a trip to **Munich Residenz**. This is where the elite, like dukes and kings, once resided. It also served as the seat of government. Initially designed as a castle, Munich Residenz was eventually transformed into a beautiful palace and showplace. Tourists from around the world are awed by the majestic splendor and opulence of the interiors, exteriors and gardens. The tour is self-guided so you can go at your own pace. It can take you up to 4-hours to make your way around the entire palace.

Although not an authentic German dining experience, we highly recommend you grab a bit to eat at the lovely **Monsoon Lehel**, an authentic Vietnamese restaurant with European style and sophistication (check out their website for a musical treat!). This is a great place to relax after a long day of touring Munich Residenz.

After you've rested a bit, we suggest checking out **Church of Our Lady**, an architectural gem that houses centuries of stories handed through the ages. It's probably the most famous landmark in Munich and shouldn't be missed.

For dinner this evening, we recommend dining at **Les Deux**. Their presentation is so gorgeous, you won't even want to eat the delicious food!

Location Information:

Munich Residenz
Address: Residenzstraße 1, 80333, Munich
Phone Number: +49 89 290 671
http://www.residenz-muenchen.de/englisch/residenc/index.htm

Monsoon Lehel
Address: Bruderstraße 6, 80538, Munich
Phone Number: +49 89 12 191 192
http://www.monsoonrestaurant-lehel.de

Church of Our Lady
Address: Frauenkirche 12, 80331, Munich
Phone Number: +49 89 290 082
http://www.muenchner-dom.de/startseite.html and
http://www.bavaria.us/church-of-our-lady-in-munich-dom-muenchen-frauenkirche-bavaria

Les Deux
Address: Maffeistrasse 3 a, 80333, Munich
Phone Number: +49 89 710 407 373
http://www.lesdeux-muc.de

• Day 4 •

Today we suggest being an early riser so you can get a jump on the day. Since you've seen a good deal of the Munich by now, you can certainly appreciate how truly beautiful it is. There's natural beauty all around.

Instead of having breakfast at the hotel, why not pack up some breakfast and lunch items from a nearby market and take them along to **The English Garden**, the beautiful and large city park. It offers amazing city views with plenty to do to keep busy. In addition to picnicking, guests can enjoy leisurely strolls, cycling, jogging, playing soccer or even renting a boat. If you haven't already had the opportunity to visit one of the cities many beer gardens now is your chance. The English Garden has four beer tents in addition to several tea tasting tents.

After spending the morning and possibly part of the afternoon hanging out at the English Garden, next visit the **BMW Museum**. Learn about the history of BMW and how it has evolved into the luxury brand it is today. There are both temporary and permanent car expositions that will simply amaze you.

After the tour, dinner may well be in order. There are plenty of options in **BMW World** to satisfy your dining preferences, casual or formal. We recommend heading to the marvelous **EssZimmer** for a wonderful selection of delectable international cuisine!

Location Information:

The English Garden
Address: Englischer Garten, 80538, Munich
Phone Number: +49 89 38 666 390
http://www.muenchen.de/sehenswuerdigkeiten/orte/120242.html

BMW Museum
Address: Am Olympiapark 2, 80809, Munich
Phone Number: +49 89 125 016 001
http://www.bmw-welt.com/en/visitor_information/guided_tours/museum.html

EssZimmer
Address: Am Olympiapark 1, 80809, Munich
Phone Number: +49 89 358 991 814
http://esszimmer-muenchen.de/en

• Day 5 •

If this is your last day in Munich, let's ensure it's as exciting as the day you arrived. Today, let's visit the interactive and informative **German Museum**. The German Museum is astoundingly the most expansive technology and science museum in the world—a *must* for any Munich itinerary!

For a nice lunch, head to the nearby **Sun City**, a restaurant that serves up fabulous Indian food in Munich.

Next, visit **St. Peter's Church**, which has the distinction of being the oldest church in Munich, built in the 11th century. The inside is a remarkable sight! Find out about the history of Munich and the Roman Catholic Church with a brief visit to St. Peter's Church.

Finally, if you enjoy more **modern attractions**, don't miss the **Pinakothek der Moderne**, Munich's amazing museum for modern arts, on center stage in the city center. We really think you'll enjoy the unique artistry and sculptures displayed at Pinakothek Der Moderne.

For a scrumptious meal this evening, the nearby **Grillin' Me Softly** is Munich street food at its finest. They really do serve up the best burgers we've ever tasted in the city—enjoy!

Location Information:

German Museum
Address: Museumsinsel 1, 80538, Munich
Phone Number: +49 89 21 791
http://www.deutsches-museum.de/en

Sun City Restaurant & Bar
Address: Erhardstrasse, 80469, Munich
Phone Number: +49 89 54 843 903
http://www.suncity-restaurant.de

St. Peter's Church
Address: Petersplatz 1, 80331, Munich
Phone Number: +49 89 21 023 7760
https://www.erzbistum-
muenchen.de/Pfarrei/Page016687.aspx

The Pinakothek Der Moderne
Address: Barer Str. 40, 80333, Munich
Phone Number: +49 89 23 805 360
http://www.pinakothek.de/en/home

Grillin' Me Softly
Address: Barerstrasse 34, 80333, Munich
Phone Number: +49 175 62 92 786
http://grillin.me

• Best Places For Travelers on a Budget •

When going on vacation, most of us want to see just how far we can stretch our money. If you're on a budget in Munich, we have some **fantastic bargain recommendations** ahead.

Bargain Munich Sleeps

One of out top picks for budget friendly accommodations in Munich is **The 4You Hostel & Hotel**. The **location is excellent**, right in the city center and bike rentals are available. The dorm rooms here are **unisex** but bathrooms are separate. Guests inclined to spend a bit more on a room are welcome to stay in one the hostel's **private rooms with their own bath-**

room and television. You get a complimentary buffet breakfast and karaoke is a part of their weekly entertainment.

Location Info:

4You Hostel & Hotel Munich
Address: Hirtenstraße 18, 80335, Munich
Phone Number: +49 89 55 21 66 0
http://www.the4you-hostels.com/en/munich

Apartments Lindwurm 70 is a great choice for an affordable rate. Just a few short stops from **Marienplatz** by bus, the location is quite ideal. Rooms are equipped with a small kitchenette, showers and essentials. Some rooms even have a **balcony**. Breakfast isn't provided but the price of the hotel, and the location, make up for it.

Location Info:

Apartments Lindwurm 70
Address: Lindwurmstrasse 70, 80337, Munich
Phone Number: +49 89 74 118 579
http://a1-apartments-lindwurm70.munichgermanyhotel.net/en

If you want something both inexpensive and **unique**, have we got something for you: **The Tent Munich** hostel. These tents are in a suburban park and can easily be accessed by way of the **Botanischer Garten** tram station or the BMW Museum. There are **specific rules** but it's well worth it, considering how **inexpensive** the accommodations are. There are shared bathrooms, a kitchen, a cafeteria, weekly cookouts and even their very own beer garden. The Tent Munich offers its guests plenty of amenities to make their stay memorable.

Location Info:

The Tent Munich
Address: In den Kirschen 30, 80992, Munich
Phone Number: +49 89 141 4300
http://www.the-tent.com

Bargain Munich Eats

For a scrumptious yet affordable dinner, we highly recommend getting over to **Viktualienmarkt** where you find more **fresh food options** than you know what to do with! The food market sits in the center of the square and is open every day. The stalls offer some of the best and **most affordable food** in the area. You can get some of Munich's most popular foods for **under €3**. We would say Viktualienmarkt is definitely the place to be if you're on a budget.

Location Info:

Viktualienmarkt
Address: Viktualienmarkt 3, 80331, Munich
Phone Number: +49 89 89 068 205
http://www.muenchen.de/int/en/shopping/markets/viktualienmarkt.html

If you ask the locals where you can eat healthy food on a budget, most will direct you to **Dean & David**.

At Dean & David you can choose to **'create your own salads,'** and try **delicious soups, sandwiches and smoothies.** The salads are really big and are a great value. With multiple locations in Munich, you're actually never far from a Dean & David restaurant.

Location Info:

Dean & David
Address: Fünf Höfe, Munich
https://deananddavid.de/en

When you'd like authentic German food at a really inexpensive price, check out **Steinheil 16**. They're known for having the **best Schnitzel** in Germany, and we definitely agree! This friendly and laid-back ambiance helps you settle right into German culture. There are also other **Bavarian food options** offered on the menu, like delicious Augustiner-Bräu beer.

Location Info:

Steinheil 16
Address: Steinheilstrasse 16, 80333, Munich
Phone Number: +49 89 527 488

• Best Places For Ultimate Luxury •

Luxury Munich Sleeps

Rooms at angelo Hotel Munich Leuchtenbergring, one of our favorite luxury hotels in Munich, are on the smaller side but are very well appointed and super comfortable. Guest rooms include a free mini-bar and breakfast is a plus, as it offers both cold and hot food items. The hotel staff is **extremely accommodating**.

Location Info:

angelo Hotel Munich Leuchtenbergring
Address: Leuchtenbergring 20, 81677, Munich
Phone Number: +49 89 189 086 0
http://www.vi-hotels.com/de/angelo-leuchtenbergring

Schiller 5 Hotel & Boardinghouse is one the best and most recommended luxury hotels in all of Munich. It's modern with all the **amenities** you expect from a hotel of this caliber. The staff is top notch and there is a **notable breakfast** served here with a wide variety to choose from. The location is wonderful since it is **in walking distance** of a lot of restaurants and specialty shops.

Location Info:

Schiller 5 Hotel & Boardinghouse
Address: Schillerstrasse 5, 80336, Munich
Phone Number: +49 89 515040
http://www.schiller5.com/index.php

The well-trained and accommodating staff of **Sofitel Munich Bayerpost** is guaranteed to exceed your expectations. Just sit back and enjoy the **elegant interiors**, the luxurious furnishings and the **star treatment**. They have everything under control. When staying here, just remember to play your part by **dressing appropriately**. No jeans and sneakers-please!

Location Info:

Sofitel Munich Bayerpost
Address: Bayerstrasse 12, 80335, Munich
Phone Number: +49 89 599 480
http://www.sofitel-munich.com/en

Luxury Munich Eats

Just about everyone loves to dine at the **Salt Restaurant**. Everything about Salt is good from the word 'go.' The meals are **artfully created** and **delicious**; they offer an extensive wine list with selections suited for the most **distinguished tastes**. The food is great, but we also love the **contemporary atmosphere** here! As with most high-end restaurants, be sure to **call ahead for reservations**.

Location Info:

Salt Restaurant
Address: Rundfunkplatz 4, 80335, Munich
Phone Number: +49 89 89 083 695
http://saltrestaurant.de

At **Fleming's Brasserie & Wine Bar**, we always appreciate the **quality of the food** and the **size of the portions**! While most patrons are certainly not looking for cheap eats, they certainly get their **money's worth in Munich** dining at Fleming's. Located in the **Fleming's Hotel**, the service is great and the staff is notably friendly and kind.

Location Info:

Fleming's Brasserie & Wine Bar
Address: Leopoldstraße 130-132, 80804, Munich
Phone Number: +49 89 206 090 0
http://www.flemings-hotels.com/en/hotels-residences/munich/flemings-hotel-muenchen-schwabing/restaurant.html

And fine dining doesn't get any better than you'll enjoy at the **Königshof Gourmet Restaurant.** This Michelin Star restaurant is a must if you'd like to spare no expense in Munich. Even if you must, saving up for an evening here is well worth it. Located in the wonderful **Hotel Königshof**, the modern European food served is some of the best we've enjoyed in all of Europe! Don't take our word — try it for yourself. You can thank us later.

Location Info:

Königshof Gourmet Restaurant
Address: Karlsplatz 25, 80335, Munich
Phone Number: +49 89 55 135 0
http://www.koenigshof-hotel.de/en/restaurants-bars/restaurant-koenigshof.html

• Munich Nightlife •

Great Bars in Munich

Like Gin? Couch Club is the place for you. They have more than 120 varieties of gin in stock with generous gin samples. They also offer an **array of cocktails** besides gin. This bar is also a favorite amongst locals and visitors.

Location Info:

Couch Club
Address: Klenzestr. 89, 80469, Munich
Phone Number: +49 89 125 55 778
http://couch-club.org

Just as inviting as its sister bar, Couch Club, **Nieder Lassing** offers the same great quality of drinks in a similar environment. When you stop in after a long day of sightseeing, you can expect creative, well prepared cocktails, comfortable sofas and the perfect mix of music for a sweet vibe in the atmosphere.

Location Info:

Nieder Lassung
Address: Buttermelcherstr. 6, 80469, Munich
Phone Number: +49 89 32 600 307
http://niederlassung.org

Great Clubs in Munich

Harry Klein is arguably one of the **best nightclubs** in Munich, if you enjoy house, techno and electronic hits. Everything about this club is perfect, from the **dynamite lighting** to the DJ. The management of Harry Klein must be doing something right because they attract crowds and crowds of visitors.

Location Info:

Harry Klein
Address: Sonnenstrasse 8, 80331, Munich
Phone Number: +49 89 40 287 400
http://harrykleinclub.de

Another favorite clubbing spot is Bob Beaman Music Club, a truly late night haunt, so make sure you're prepared to sleep in! The location is quite **inconspicuous**, which is actually part of its appeal. **Great drinks** and **good music** await you at Bob Beaman's.

Location Info:

Bob Beaman Music Club
Address: Gabelsbergerstrasse 4, 80333, Munich
Phone Number: +49 177 254 7476
http://bobbeamanclub.com

Great Live Music in Munich

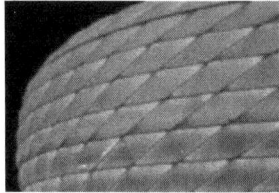

The Jazz Club Unterfahrt welcomes local musicians and internationally acclaimed jazz artists and also doubles as an **art gallery**. When visiting Jazzclub Unterfahrt you can dine on a variety of international food options, while listening to truly **amazing jazz in an intimate setting** we really like.

Location Info:

Jazz Club Unterfahrt
Address: Einsteinstraße 42, 81675, Munich
Phone Number: +49 89 448 2794
http://www.unterfahrt.de/index.php?language=en

You can also listen to smooth sounds at **Bayerische Staatsoper** (Bavarian State Opera House), **an amazing venue with a rich history**. Visit their website and go to the concert section for upcoming performances during your visit.

Location Info:

Bayerische Staatsoper
Address: Max-Joseph-Platz 2, 80539, Munich
Phone Number: +49 89 21 85 01
https://www.staatsoper.de/en/index.html

Great Theatre in Munich

Make plans to see a show at GOP Varieté-Theatre München. You can experience magic and comedy, acrobatics and more. The theater also houses a **European restaurant.** If you want **a night full of fun and excitement**, visit GOP Varieté-Theatre München.

Location Info:

GOP Varieté-Theatre München
Address: Maximilianstraße 47, 80538, Munich
Phone Number: +49 89 210 288 444
http://www.variete.de/en/venues/munich/munich.html

Productions at the Deutsches Theater are among the most popular in state. Set in a 19th century theatre, it stands alone as a major player in the **world of theatrics** in Munich. With regularly scheduled **international musical artists** and shows, there's sure to be a performance worth checking out during your stay.

Location Info:

Deutsches Theater
Address: Schwanthalerstraße 13, 80336, Munich
Phone Number: +49 30 28 441 225
https://www.deutschestheater.de/en

• Conclusion •

When planning a trip to **Munich**, it might be nice to know there's much more to the city than just Oktoberfest and bratwurst! So if you're interested in **culture, architecture and history**, we believe Munich will prove a lovely city to discover and explore.

As you can tell from our guide, Munich is a city for everyone, both young and old. You can bring the entire family along for the ride of discovering something old, new and fascinating.

So we hope you have found our guide to the esteemed city of Munich helpful and wish you a safe, interesting, and fun-filled trip to Germany!

Warmest regards,

The Passport to European Travel Guides Team

Visit our Blog! Grab more of our signature guides for all your travel needs!

http://www.passporttoeuropeantravelguides.blogspot.com

★ **Join our mailing list** ★ to follow our Travel Guide Series. You'll be automatically entered for a chance to win a **$100 Visa Gift Card** in our monthly drawings! Be sure to respond to the confirmation e-mail to complete the subscription

• About the Authors •

PASSPORT TO
European Travel
The Best Travel Guides to Europe!

Passport to European Travel Guides is an eclectic team of international jet setters who know exactly what travelers and tourists want in a cut-to-the-chase, comprehensive travel guide that suits a wide range of budgets.

Our growing collection of distinguished European travel guides are guaranteed to give first-hand insight to each locale, complete with day-to-day, guided itineraries you won't want to miss!

We want our brand to be your official Passport to European Travel — one you can always count on!

Bon Voyage!

The Passport to European Travel Guides Team

http://www.passporttoeuropeantravelguides.blogspot.com

Printed in Great Britain
by Amazon